GREAT
BUILDING
FEATS

THE GREAT WALL OF CHINA

LESLEY A. DuTEMPLE

Lerner Publications Company
Minneapolis

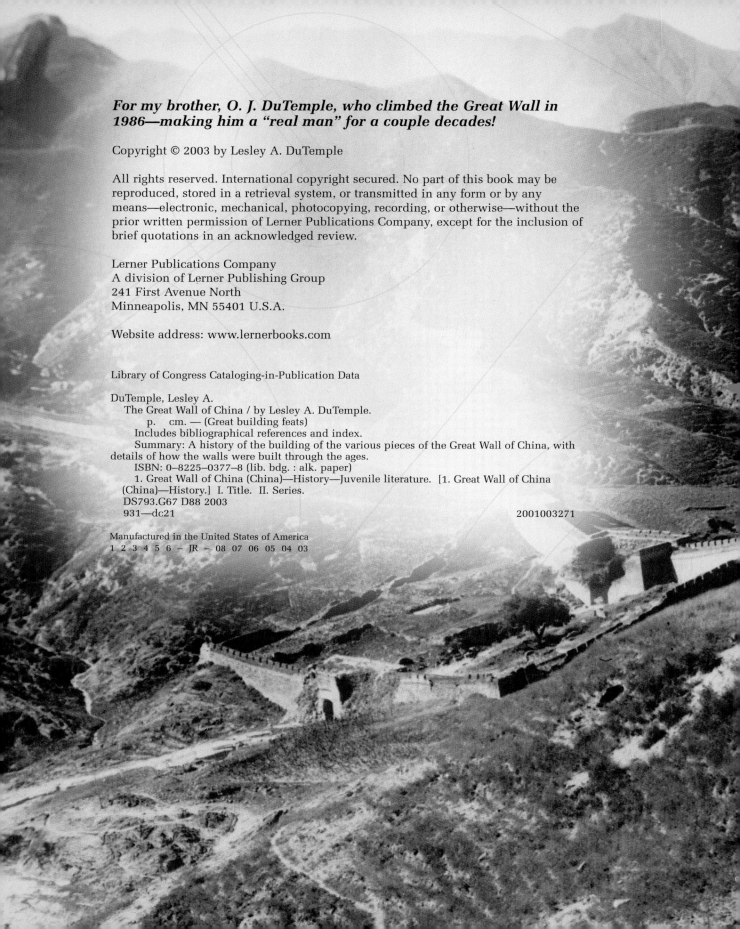

For my brother, O. J. DuTemple, who climbed the Great Wall in 1986—making him a "real man" for a couple decades!

Lerner Publications Company
A division of Lerner Publishing Group
241 First Avenue North
Minneapolis, MN 55401 U.S.A.

Website address: www.lernerbooks.com

Library of Congress Cataloging-in-Publication Data

DuTemple, Lesley A.
    The Great Wall of China / by Lesley A. DuTemple.
        p.   cm. — (Great building feats)
    Includes bibliographical references and index.
    Summary: A history of the building of the various pieces of the Great Wall of China, with details of how the walls were built through the ages.
    ISBN: 0–8225–0377–8 (lib. bdg. : alk. paper)
    1. Great Wall of China (China)—History—Juvenile literature. [1. Great Wall of China (China)—History.] I. Title. II. Series.
    DS793.G67 D88 2003
    931—dc21   2001003271

Manufactured in the United States of America
1 2 3 4 5 6 – JR – 08 07 06 05 04 03

CONTENTS

ABOUT GREAT BUILDING FEATS

HUMANS HAVE LONG SOUGHT to make their mark on the world. From the ancient Great Wall of China to the ultramodern Channel Tunnel linking Britain and France, grand structures reveal how people have tried to express themselves and to better their lives.

Great structures have served a number of purposes. Sometimes they met a practical need. For example, the New York subway system made getting around a huge city easier. Other structures reflected spiritual beliefs. The Pantheon in Rome, Italy, was created as a temple to Roman gods and later became a Roman Catholic church. Sometimes we can only guess at the story behind a structure. The purpose of Stonehenge in England eludes us, and perhaps it always will.

The Great Wall snakes across mountains, valleys, and deserts. It is a magnificent sight and a truly great building feat.

This book is one in a series of books called Great Building Feats. Each book in the series takes a close look at one of the most amazing building feats around the world. Each feat posed a unique set of engineering and geographical problems. In many cases, these problems seemed nearly insurmountable when construction began.

More than a compilation of facts, the Great Building Feats series not only describes how each structure was built, but also why. Each project called forth the best minds of its time. Many people invested their all in the outcome. Their lives are as much a part of the structure as the earth and stone used in its construction.

Finally, each structure in the Great Building Feats series remains a dynamic feature of the modern world, still amazing users and viewers as well as historians.

THE GREAT WALL

It is impossible to write about the Great Wall of China without writing about the history of China, for the two are closely linked. Building the wall involved a good part of the Chinese population at various periods for nearly two thousand years. In fact, the Great Wall isn't really one wall at all, but a series of walls built and rebuilt by different emperors. There's the Great Wall of the Qin dynasty, and the Great Wall of the Han dynasty, and the Great Wall of the Ming dynasty, and many others in between.

Most of the workers on the wall did not participate willingly, and more than one million of them died during the building of the first Great Wall. But China needed a wall across its northern border if it was to survive as a nation.

For centuries, nomadic tribes inhabited the regions north of China. There were no effective geographical barriers to keep them out, and China constantly had to defend itself against the attacks of people they considered barbarians. So China's first emperor hit upon the idea of building a wall to stop them from raiding the country.

The Great Wall not only kept invaders out, but it also kept the Chinese people in. Living in relative isolation, they developed one of the world's greatest civilizations. The Great Wall of China provides a vivid portrait—"painted" with earth, bricks, and stone—of their way of thinking.

Although the wall started as a royal project, it has managed to survive long after the downfall of China's imperial dynasties. As a modern defensive military structure, the Great Wall is useless. But it serves as a powerful reminder of two thousand years of political unrest and social turmoil. And it remains an important symbol of past accomplishments, national pride, and patriotism—a great building feat that has defined a nation.

China is the largest country in Asia. Great rivers flow through fertile farmland. High mountains, dry grasslands, and vast deserts lie to the north and west.

HADRIAN'S WALL

The Chinese might have been the first, but other cultures built defensive walls, too. One of the most famous was erected under a Roman emperor.

Hadrian ruled the Roman Empire from A.D. 117 through A.D. 138, when it stretched across Europe and into England. In what would become Germany, Hadrian built wooden walls along the Rhine River to keep out the Germanic tribes. But Hadrian's greatest wall-building effort occurred in what became England, which was the northernmost outpost of the Roman Empire.

To protect his empire from the barbarian tribes in the north, Hadrian built a wall that was roughly 10 feet (3 meters) wide and 12 feet (3.7 m) high and stretched for 73 miles (117 kilometers) across the entire width of England.

Hadrian's Wall *(below)* took only six years to build and was constructed by Roman soldiers—all of whom were paid for their service. Most of the wall was built from stone, but portions were constructed from turf, a type of earth with so much decayed vegetation in it that it can be burned like wood.

Hadrian might have known about the walls built nearly five hundred years earlier by the Chinese. His wall is remarkably similar in its design. Like the Great Wall, Hadrian's Wall contained forts, towers, housing for soldiers, built-in gates for traveling to either side, and protected positions for soldiers guarding it. Hadrian's Wall still exists and can be visited.

Chapter One
WHY A WALL?

(4000 B.C.–500 B.C.)

ALMOST EVERYONE HAS HEARD about the Great Wall of China. Thousands of tourists visit it every day. No other structure made by humans is larger.

But the Great Wall isn't the only enormous wall built by the Chinese people. It's just the latest and largest in a series of walls. Thousands of years before construction on this Great Wall even started, the Chinese were building walls. No other people have built so many.

DIFFERENT GEOGRAPHY, DIFFERENT LIFESTYLES

In ancient times, the area we refer to as China was occupied by several small tribes of hunter-gatherers. At least seven thousand years ago, they roamed the land, following the wild animals that provided

Above: Early Chinese people settled in the fertile river valleys and took up farming. This ancient carved brick depicts them working in the fields. *Right:* Mountains and hills divide the fertile farmland from the dry grasslands to the north.

them with food and clothing. They dressed in animal skins, probably lived in caves, and had no written language.

About 4000 B.C. (six thousand years ago), some of these tribes began changing the way they lived. Instead of following herds of animals and moving with the change of seasons, they tamed some of these animals, settled down, and began planting crops. As more of these small groups settled in the same fertile areas, small villages sprang up. Gradually, as more villages developed in each region, the regions developed into separate states.

But not every tribe gave up its nomadic wanderings and settled into an agricultural way of life. Some tribes continued to be nomadic. China's enormously varied geography promoted this separation.

The northwestern part of China is a land of dry, sandy deserts. This region gradually gives way to arid steppes (dry grassland areas) where wild animals graze. In the central and southern parts of China, rich fertile plains stretch out endlessly from giant rivers that flow across the country. The northern and southern parts of the country are divided from each other by hills and mountain ranges that stretch from the Yellow Sea in the east all the way through the Gobi Desert in the west.

The geography of each region determined the way of life of the tribes that lived there. Those who settled on the plains along the Huang (Yellow) River developed agriculture. The land there was flat, fertile, and well watered, a perfect place to grow crops and raise animals.

The tribes who stayed in the arid steppes and mountainous regions of the north found the area was too dry for farming. They continued their nomadic way of life.

EARLY WALLS

The nomadic tribes of the north couldn't help but notice, and envy, the riches of their southern neighbors. After settling into an agricultural way of life, the southern tribes were able to grow enough food to feed the community. They grew crops, harvested them, and stored the excess until the next planting season. Unlike the northern nomadic tribes, they didn't have to go looking for their next meal.

With no mountains high enough to present real barriers between the regions, the northern tribes began raiding the settled southern tribes. The northerners had horses and weapons, which gave them the advantage in their raids.

The Xiongnu, the Chinese name for the northern nomadic herders, rode south to raid Chinese farms and villages.

This is part of an early wall built to protect a Chinese village from attack.

China's first walls were built by agricultural villages to keep out aggressive or greedy neighbors as well as raiders from the north. Even if a wall didn't completely stop the raiding, the time it took the enemy to scale the wall, or break through, or ride around it, gave the southern farmers the chance to arm themselves and fight back or to flee.

Archaeologists have uncovered several of these ancient walls, and they believe that many early villages had walls around them. Even after China was unified and peaceful, invaders from the north kept coming for the next 5,500 years. The Chinese kept building walls to protect themselves.

BUILDING AN EARLY WALL

It's easy to take wall building for granted. Humans build walls all the time. There are walls around school playgrounds and walls around baseball fields. There are even walls, or fences, between homes. Some industries do nothing but manufacture walls and the materials used to build them.

In modern times, people use machinery to build big walls. Bulldozers dig out the earth for a wall's foundation, and giant cranes lift

WHAT IS A WALL?

A wall is an upright barrier. It might be constructed to keep creatures in or to keep out weather or intruders. Stones roughly stacked across the entrance of a cave during prehistoric times qualify as a wall.

Walls can be built from any number of things. Rocks, logs, wooden planks, bamboo poles, woven mats, cut stone, concrete, plaster, and steel are some.

Walls can stand alone, like the Great Wall. Or they can be part of a structure, such as a house wall. The engineering principles that keep it upright remain the same.

The higher a wall, the more weight is carried by the lower part of it. Weight pushes down, but it also pushes out, so materials used for building a wall must be strong enough to absorb weight without bulging at the sides. For example, clay can hold its own weight and stand up straight, but it can't absorb much more extra weight. Extra weight makes the clay bulge outward so much that it completely flattens. But when extra weight is applied to a rock, the rock holds firm.

Different materials have different strengths. Rocks and steel are usually the strongest materials and can hold the most weight. Wood is fairly strong. Surprisingly, dirt can also absorb a lot of weight, particularly if it is packed tightly enough to rid it of all air spaces. Like clay, it will flatten, but once flat, it is strong.

The center line through a wall must be absolutely straight. If the top of the wall isn't perfectly aligned with the bottom, the wall will topple. One solution is to make the bottom of the wall thicker than the top. This works well for a freestanding wall, but it won't work for walls that meet at corners, such as the walls in a house. The Great Wall was designed to be thicker at the bottom than at the top to make sure it would stand firmly.

construction materials into place. Cement mixers pour concrete. Even bricks are delivered by a mechanical forklift.

China's great walls were between 20 and 30 feet (6 and 9 m) wide and about 30 feet (9 m) tall, as high as a three-story building, and they were built entirely by hand. Even the newest sections of the Great Wall were built long before cement mixers, cranes, and trucks were invented. These early wall builders had handmade buckets, slats of wood and bamboo, piles of dirt, pounding sticks, and their own hands. When the first Great Wall was constructed, there weren't even any wheelbarrows. Over the course of the two thousand years the Great Wall of China was under construction, rulers, workers, and circumstances changed—but the primary methods of construction remained the same.

4,000 MILES—ONE CONSTRUCTION METHOD

The Great Wall stretches for more than 4,000 miles (6,450 km) across China's northern border. In North America, that's the distance from the southern tip of Florida to the North Pole. In addition, smaller walls branch off the main wall. The longest of these is no more than 100 miles (160 km) long. Most measurements of the Great Wall include these side walls.

Nobody really knows the true length of the wall. To date, no single person has traveled all of it. But new technology, like satellite photography, has

Radar images clearly show the Great Wall. About 93 miles (150 km) of wall is visible in this image. The two dark ovals are dry lake beds, and the rectangles are farmers' fields.

enabled historians to rediscover more than 800 miles (1,287 km) of buried wall.

From what historians can see, only one construction method was used in building the wall. *Hang-tu,* the technique of constructing walls out of packed earth, was developed in ancient times, and this ancient method was used to build most of the Great Wall. Even where the Great Wall appears to be made of brick, the bricks are only a facade. Underneath is a hang-tu wall.

ANCIENT METHODS FOR NEWER WALLS

The name *hang-tu* comes from two separate Chinese words. *Hang* means "beaten," or "pounded down." *Tu* translates roughly as "earth." Walls constructed by the hang-tu method are walls that are gradually built up by stamping and pounding dirt into compact layers.

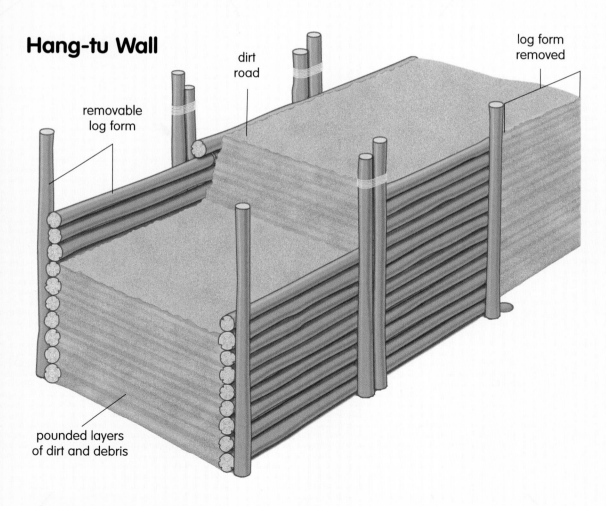

Hang-tu Wall

dirt road

log form removed

removable log form

pounded layers of dirt and debris

To build a hang-tu wall, workers first built a form, usually out of wood or bamboo, the sides as far apart as the planned width of the wall. For instance, if the wall was going to be 5 feet (1.5 m) thick, the workers would build the forms 5 feet (1.5 m) apart.

The next step was to dump dirt into the forms. Workers then stamped on the dirt, or used some type of pounding tool, to pack it down and remove air pockets. Hang-tu walls were built up layer by layer, and each layer was usually only a few inches thick. Once a layer was packed tightly, it could hold a lot of weight—more weight than a wooden wall. As each layer was finished, more dirt was dumped in and packed down. Even in later walls, the thickest layer of dirt was usually no more than 8 inches (20 centimeters) deep.

Packing each layer tightly before starting the next layer ensured that the wall wouldn't settle, or sink. When the wall reached the desired height, the wooden forms were pulled away. What remained was a strong, stable wall. A hang-tu wall.

All of China's very early walls were built using the hang-tu method. And almost six thousand years later, when work ended on the Great Wall, the hang-tu method was still in use.

DEFINING A CULTURE WITH WALLS

Walls can serve more than one purpose. They're usually built to keep things out, but they also keep things in. A Chinese village with a wall around it (or a country with a wall around it), might keep invaders out, but it would also keep its citizens in. Their world would be determined by life within those walls.

All of China's walls, from the early ones to the Great Wall, did this. They were helpful in repelling invasions, but they also kept the Chinese people isolated, living in their own world and controlled by their ruler. The Great Wall allowed China to develop a unique culture. For many centuries, all of China's walls reflected government policy: Invaders stay out, Chinese people stay in.

To the Chinese, their land and civilization were at the center of the universe. Anyone who wasn't Chinese was a barbarian and unworthy to participate in Chinese culture. The Great Wall kept these "inferior" people at bay and kept the Chinese in China. This allowed the Chinese emperor to control and tax trade between China and the northern barbarian tribes.

CHINA'S EARLIEST WALLS

For all of its rich history and ancient archaeological sites, much of China remains a mystery to people of the outside world. During most of the 1900s, there was a surge of interest in archaeology in the Western world and in excavating ancient sites and reconstructing past civilizations. While archaeologists were busy investigating ancient life in other areas around the globe, China was a closed country. The Chinese government allowed few foreigners into the country and funded little work by Chinese archaeologists. This is one reason why the Great Wall has never been completely unearthed or surveyed.

Recently, however, China has been much more willing to let archaeological teams work on sites in the country. In the present-day province of Shaanxi, archaeologists have unearthed the remains of several ancient walls built around 4000 B.C.

One of the walls is exceedingly well preserved. It stood 20 feet (6 m) high and was roughly 27 feet (8.2 m) wide at the top and a little over 1,300 feet (400 m) long. It originally surrounded an entire village. It is a hang-tu wall. Archaeologists are hoping that further study at the site will help them to learn more about early Chinese people.

Chinese archaeologists are rediscovering their country's ancient history. This mummy of an important wealthy woman was found in 2001. She is wearing several layers of silk, a gold crown, and five jeweled rings.

This Chinese attitude of superiority didn't just apply to the barbarians of the north. Different areas of China began putting up walls to keep out other Chinese, too. Some groups considered themselves more Chinese than others, so they wanted to keep the inferior others out of their region. As the Chinese groups themselves grew more and more diverse, disputes and clashes arose among them. From these battles came the beginnings of the Great Wall.

Chapter Two
MANY STATES, MANY WALLS

(500 B.C.–221 B.C.)

HISTORIANS KNOW A LOT about China's early history because the Chinese developed a written language about 3,000 years ago. While other ancient cultures passed along their history through oral storytelling, China's history was being written down.

STRUGGLES FOR POWER

By 600 B.C., or about 2,600 years ago, China was divided into at least a dozen independent states ruled by kings. The kings fought with each other, and, if they lived in the northern regions of China, they also fought with the northern barbarians.

Soldiers are attacking a walled city in this scene on a bronze vessel from the Warring States Period.

China's geography is so diverse that different states possessed different resources. This meant that one state controlled the navigation of a river, while another controlled deposits of iron, and another controlled the best farmland, or a strategic mountain pass. Most kings fought to acquire for themselves the advantages another state possessed.

It wasn't long before the strongest of these kings wanted to unite all the states of China and become emperor of them all. For them this meant being emperor of the world. The world outside China didn't count.

THE WARRING STATES PERIOD

The fighting to control all of China reached its peak around 475 B.C., about 2,500 years ago, and continued until 221 B.C. The fighting was so furious that historians refer to these 254 years as the Warring States Period.

The Warring States Period is called that because that's what it was— outright war among the Chinese states. Before 475 B.C., fights among

states had usually lasted only a day or so. But during the Warring States Period, the squabbles turned into real battles that lasted for weeks or even months. Hundreds of thousands of soldiers fought, and whole states came under siege.

Just as the battles grew longer, so did the walls. Before 475 B.C., Chinese walls were no more than 20 miles (32 km) long. But starting in 475 B.C., most Chinese states began constructing longer walls that stretched for hundreds of miles along their borders to protect them from neighboring states.

The warring states built walls to protect themselves from attacks from neighboring states, as well as from raids by northern nomads.

Chu was the first state to construct a large defensive wall system. Chu's king ordered a 300-mile-long (483-km-long) wall built along the northern border to keep out any barbarians that might come in, as well as any unwanted Chinese neighbors.

Other Chinese states quickly followed Chu's example. The state of Qi built the next giant wall.

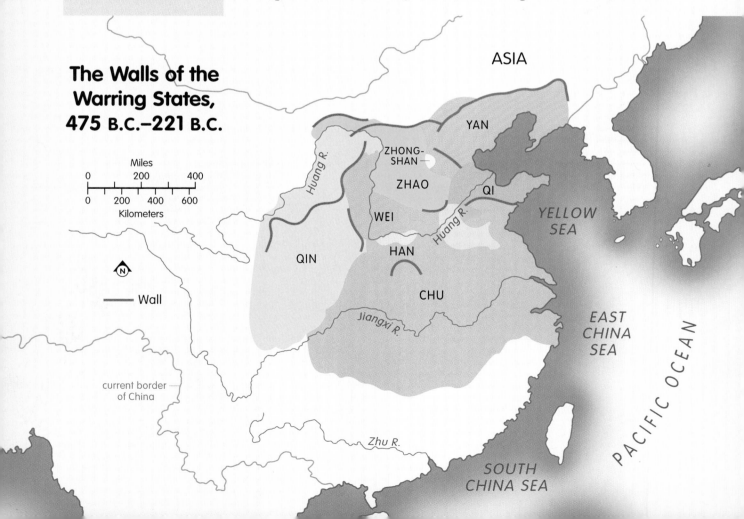

The Walls of the Warring States, 475 B.C.–221 B.C.

Miles
0   200   400
0   200   400   600
Kilometers

N

— Wall

current border of China

ASIA

YAN

ZHONG-SHAN

Huang R.

ZHAO

WEI

QI

Huang R.

HAN

YELLOW SEA

QIN

CHU

Jiangxi R.

EAST CHINA SEA

PACIFIC OCEAN

Zhu R.

SOUTH CHINA SEA

The ancient states of Zhongshan, Wei, and Zhao also built walls that ran for hundreds of miles.

CHINA TO THE WINNER

The fighting couldn't continue forever. One king was bound to emerge victorious. During the Warring States Period, a handful of states grew more powerful through alliances with other states and with barbarian tribes—and through treachery and deceit. Eventually Qi, Chu, Han, Zhao, Wei, Yan, and Qin became the most powerful states in China. These states built enormous walls, walls that stretched even farther than before.

By the 300s B.C., the states of Chu in the south and Qin in the northwest were battling to control all of China. By 312 B.C., Qin had begun a long, relentless campaign to gain control of all of China. In 246 B.C., a fourteen-year-old boy named Zheng became the king of Qin. Zheng was a ruthless fighter, and by 221 B.C., Qin had conquered all the other states. Zheng became the first emperor of all of China.

Zheng was determined to remain the supreme emperor of all of China forever. No one would invade his nation or conquer him. A wall had kept the state of Qin safe. Surely an even bigger wall would keep all of China safe. Zheng decided to build that wall: a great wall.

WHAT'S IN A NAME?

The English language uses an alphabet of twenty-six letters. Each letter has a sound that is assigned to it, such as "b" for the sound "buh." By mixing and combining twenty-six letters, words are formed. Chinese writing doesn't use symbols to represent a particular sound. In Chinese, a symbol usually represents an entire word or idea. For instance, instead of combining letter symbols such as h-o-u-s-e, for "house," Chinese writing uses just one symbol to represent the word "house."

Since Chinese and English writing are so different, there is no way to translate one into the other directly. Consequently, different translators in the past often came up with different solutions. This is the reason why you may see Chinese names written several different ways in English.

For example, the state of Qin is also referred to as Ch'in. Zheng, the king of Qin, is also referred to as Cheng and Chao Cheng. As emperor, he is referred to as Qin Shi Huangdi in this book, but he also appears as Qin Shi Huang, and Shih huang-ti among other names. Almost any English version of a Chinese name will have more than one way of spelling it—depending which book you're reading. There is an official standard spelling, called pinyin, for Chinese words. This book uses the pinyin form.

Chapter Three
ONE COUNTRY, ONE WALL
(221 B.C.–210 B.C.)

EVEN AT THE AGE OF FOUR-teen, Zheng demonstrated remarkable skills in warfare and a ruthless ambition to get what he wanted. In 221 B.C., when he proclaimed himself Qin Shi Huangdi, or First Sovereign Emperor of China, he became the ruler of the largest country on earth.

In order to unify China and control its millions of people, Qin Shi Huangdi instituted a rigid system of rules and regulations. By Qin Shi Huangdi's imperial decree, all forms of writing were standardized and so were all weights and measures and money. This made it easier to do business throughout the country.

Above: Qin Shi Huangdi standardized weights and measures to help unify his empire. This is a weight standard from the Qin dynasty. *Right:* In this ancient drawing, a Chinese general guards a gate in the Great Wall.

Qin Shi Huangdi wanted to keep a tight watch over his kingdom to prevent rebellions before they started. To do this, he needed to be able to travel safely on good roads, so he standardized the width of all highways and decreed that an elaborate network of new roads be built. But the walls constructed during the long and bloody Warring States Period stood in the way.

TEAR DOWN THE WALLS!

The obvious solution to this problem was to tear down any wall that made it difficult for the First Sovereign Emperor to travel about his own country. Barbarians, such as the Xiongnu, were still lurking about in the north, waiting to thunder down from the steppes and plunder China. The various northern walls built by the states were China's only protection against them. So Qin Shi Huangdi further decreed that the walls in the north would be left standing and linked together to form one solid barrier against the barbarians. They would be combined into one great wall.

Qin Shi Huangdi was demanding that hundreds of miles of wall be torn down and thousands of miles of new wall built. Who was going to do all this work?

EVERYONE TO WORK

Once China had developed into an organized society—at least five hundred years before Zheng became emperor—it quickly developed a class system. That is, some people were richer and more powerful than others. Some people owned large amounts of land, and other people worked for them. Some Chinese people even owned slaves. There were always more peasants, or poorer people, in China than there were rich people.

There was also a large class of intellectuals, or people who studied and taught. The intellectuals were the people who developed China's

CHINESE ORGANIZATION

The Chinese were the first culture to develop a certain system for governing and organizing large groups of people. This system, often referred to as a bureaucracy, is still used by governments, corporations, military organizations, and even schools.

Initially, the government organization took the shape of a pyramid. The king or other leader was at the top. The officials in charge of each department, such as crops, or housing, or tax collecting, were below the leader. Lesser officials helped the main officials carry out their assignments. Workers were most numerous, and they were at the bottom of the pyramid.

Starting with Qin Shi Huangdi, Chinese emperors took this initial organization and refined it further. Under the emperor were governors who headed each state, and under them, other officials who oversaw regions within the states. Throughout the country, taxes were collected in an orderly fashion by another group of officials.

The Chinese military had its own bureaucracy. The top-ranking general reported directly to the emperor. Under this general, there were other military officers who oversaw the regiments of soldiers, taught them skills, and made sure orders were carried out.

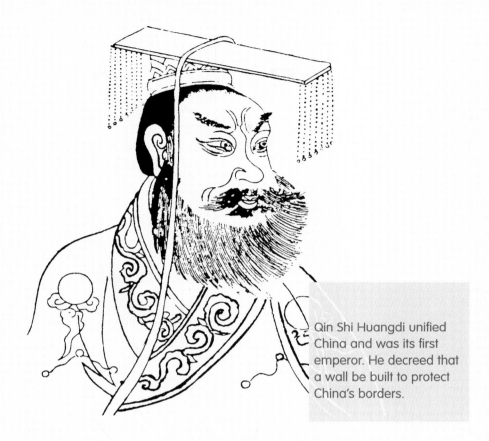

Qin Shi Huangdi unified China and was its first emperor. He decreed that a wall be built to protect China's borders.

written language, invented paper and scientific instruments, and wrote books. In many ways, the intellectuals were the people who had made China the advanced nation that it was.

To build the wall Qin Shi Huangdi wanted, everyone would have to work on it. Getting the slaves and peasants to work on the Great Wall was easy—Qin Shi Huangdi simply ordered them to do it. As emperor, he had absolute power. Anybody who didn't obey an order was executed. His power was such that he had generals in his army executed if they arrived late at their post—even when they had to march hundreds of miles through bad weather to get there. Although Qin Shi Huangdi wielded absolute power, the intellectuals dared to protest against his despotic government, and they protested mightily.

PROFESSORS WITH SHOVELS

The Chinese had two very different ideas about how people should be governed. Intellectuals believed that people were basically good and that rulers needed to be just, fair, and compassionate. Qin Shi Huangdi believed that people were basically untrustworthy, and that, as ruler, he needed to be strict and rigid to control them. As a result, he and the intellectuals were constantly at odds with each other.

But Qin Shi Huangdi had an answer to these disagreements. He made it a crime to think anything except what he thought. Consequently, the intellectuals who disagreed with him were found guilty and sentenced to years of hard labor. That hard labor was working on construction of the Great Wall. People who had never done anything more physically strenuous than read a book found themselves living in freezing, muddy camps. They spent their days hauling dirt and stones simply because they disagreed with Qin Shi Huangdi's philosophy of governing.

This is how the Great Wall got started. It wasn't a friendly community project, with everyone working together, pitching in to help keep out the barbarians. It was forced labor—forced by an authoritarian emperor whom very few people liked—done under enormous protest.

THE FIRST GREAT WALL GOES UP

Qin Shi Huangdi's method of dealing with dissidents, the people who protested his policies, was a typical example of his style of government. He took only his own advice and got what he wanted—immediately. What he wanted was a Great Wall.

But unlike the Warring States walls, which were hundreds of miles long, Qin Shi Huangdi was demanding a *wanli changchen,* a "10,000 Li Wall." (A *li* is a Chinese measurement equal to about 1,760 feet (536 m).) Qin Shi Huangdi wanted a wall that was approximately 3,000 miles (4,828 km) long. He wanted a wall that, if built in the United States, would stretch from Boston to San Francisco. All of it would be built by humans alone, without the aid of machinery.

It was clearly a formidable task. Historians believe that, at most, only a few hundred miles of preexisting Warring States walls were ever incorporated into Qin Shi Huangdi's 10,000 Li Wall. At least 2,500 miles (4,023 km) of new wall were to be built.

GENERAL MENG TIEN

Who kept everything going and organized all these humans? Constructing a great wall along China's northern border may have been Qin Shi Huangdi's idea, but emperors don't usually bother themselves with the details—they find someone else to get the job done.

THE BOOK-BURNING EMPEROR

Qin Shi Huangdi is known for a lot of things, including the development of roads, the standardization of money and measurements, and strict tyranny. He is also known as the emperor who ordered the burning of all the books in China *(below)*.

Books contain ideas, and Qin Shi Huangdi didn't want any ideas around but his own. Soldiers moved throughout the country gathering up all the books they could find and burning them on great public bonfires. The only books allowed to remain were medical books.

Fortunately for future generations and historians, many books were hidden, and Qin Shi Huangdi's reign was fairly short. After he died, books were taken out of hiding, and people began to study them again.

General Meng Tien, one of the emperor's most trusted advisers, was in charge of building 1,500 miles (2,414 km) of the Great Wall. At the same time, he commanded 300,000 soldiers who protected the wall builders and the borders.

Not a lot of written records survive from this period of Chinese history. But nearly all that do credit General Meng Tien with building more than half of this original Great Wall.

General Meng Tien was one of Qin Shi Huangdi's most trusted advisers and military commanders. Meng Tien's father had been a general for Zheng before he became the first emperor. And Meng Tien, himself, was Zheng's top-ranking military commander. Meng Tien was instrumental in helping Zheng become Qin Shi Huangdi, the First Sovereign Emperor of China.

Meng Tien organized nearly one million unhappy workers and got them to build more than 1,500 miles (2,414 km) of wall—and to do it in snow, rain, and sleet. Meanwhile, he was also fighting off barbarian invaders and was in charge of 300,000 soldiers.

Meng Tien probably wasn't any nicer than Qin Shi Huangdi, and he most certainly held the same views about controlling people. But organizing one million workers and 300,000 soldiers to do a single task is an amazing accomplishment no matter what your personality. And Meng Tien accomplished it in less than seven years. What started off as a heap of pounded dirt became one of the wonders of the world—a beautiful wall that wound like a serpent across the Chinese landscape.

BASE CAMPS AND SUPPLY ROUTES

Before starting construction on the wall, Meng Tien had to establish base camps. Base camps were places where supplies would be delivered. Each base camp also had some housing for soldiers. The workers who did the actual construction on the wall lived in temporary camps right next to the wall. The worker camps were disassembled and moved along as the wall progressed.

Meng Tien established thirty-four base camps along the route of the wall. Everything needed for

The Great Wall winds like a serpent across the mountains near Beijing, the capital of modern China.

the wall was sent out from these bases. He, the architects, the engineers, and the soldiers under his command worked out of these base camps for seven years—from approximately 217 B.C. until Qin Shi Huangdi's death in 210 B.C.

Besides base camps, Meng Tien also had to establish supply lines, or ways to get supplies to the wall. Although the wall itself was usually constructed from whatever was on hand, supplies were still needed. When the wall was being constructed through areas that had no bamboo or wood available for the hang-tu forms, it had to be delivered.

Keeping the southern supply routes open so that supplies could reach the wall was no easy task. Supply carts, pulled by horses, donkeys, or even humans, made their way northward to the construction sites. They moved slowly and were easy targets for bandits. To keep the supply lines open, soldiers had to be stationed along the routes, or accompany the supplies. Once this basic organization was accomplished, Meng Tien was ready to begin building.

Caravans of donkeys, as depicted in this ancient Chinese artwork, brought supplies through the mountains to the builders of the Great Wall.

WALL WORKERS

Intellectuals and slaves weren't the only people to work on the Great Wall. Qin Shi Huangdi ordered most of the population to work. Most of China's farmers were called away from their land, as were the peasants who worked the fields but did not own land. Convicts and prisoners were hauled out of prison and put to work. Almost any man who could walk and hold a shovel was sent to work on the wall.

Even along the wall, there was still a class system in place. Convicts and prisoners had the worst time of it. Convicts might be people who had committed a real crime, such as murder, but frequently their only crime was that they had been too poor to pay their taxes. Their heads were shaved and their faces were blackened so that everyone knew they were convicts. They were also forced to work while wearing chains.

Other workers didn't have it much better. They all were guarded by soldiers and forced to work all daylight hours. In summertime, this meant sixteen hours every day.

DEATH ALONG THE WALL

Camps were set up next to the wall for the workers, but there was never enough housing, and what there was was so poorly constructed, it didn't keep out the cold, rain, or snow. The workers had no proper blankets or beds, and most of them just slept outside on the ground. None of the worker camps had

BODIES IN THE GREAT WALL?

More than one million workers died during the construction of the Great Wall. To get an idea of how many people this is, think about an elementary school. Even the largest elementary school usually has only about five hundred students. One million people is the equivalent of roughly two thousand elementary schools. Just where were these one million bodies buried?

For centuries, the popular belief was that the bodies were buried in the wall itself. It was even said that disobedient workers were walled up alive. The Great Wall was referred to as "the longest cemetery on earth."

But historians know that this isn't true. If there were bodies in the wall, the whole structure would have collapsed long ago. The decomposing bodies would have created air pockets in the dirt and rocks, and the wall would have crumbled. The bodies of the dead workers were buried in trenches alongside the wall.

toilet facilities. Unless the wall was being built near a lake or river, workers had no clean water.

Food was always in short supply, too. Even with soldiers guarding the supply lines, bandits still attacked, and supplies rarely got through on a regular basis. Another problem was a lack of food in China itself. So many farmers and peasants were working on the wall, there weren't enough people to grow the crops. Workers received a little bowl of rice and boiled cabbage each day—if they were lucky. Sometimes there was nothing for days.

Getting this small amount of food to the workers was all the government could manage. Every other need fell by the wayside. Workers wore what they had arrived in until their clothes wore out. After that, in winter, they wore rags or animal skins. In summer, they worked naked.

There were few tools to help with the construction of Qin Shi Huangdi's 10,000 Li Wall. For this first Great Wall, workers probably used bamboo poles or narrow logs to build the hang-tu forms because they didn't have saws to cut wooden planks. The workers probably used rocks to pound the lengths of bamboo into the ground.

The Chinese knew how to work metal, so there were probably some small metal shovels available. Mostly, though, dirt was scooped by hand into woven baskets, which were then carried up ladders and dumped into the hang-tu form. The ladders were constructed from bamboo poles lashed together with woven string. This original wall didn't use much stone (the technology for cutting and moving stone hadn't been developed to any extent by the Chinese). When stones were used, workers had to heave and push them up ramps.

The wall was constructed over mountain ranges and through deserts. In the mountains, it rained or snowed for much of the year. In the desert, it was scorching hot and dry. No matter what the weather, workers toiled on day after day.

At least one million workers died while building the Great Wall for Qin Shi Huangdi. So many workers died, the emperor ran out of men. That didn't stop him, though. He ordered the widows of the dead workers to work in their late husbands' places. Many children, who had no one to care for them when their mothers left to work on the wall, died. Who knows if the Chinese people would have continued to suffer under Qin Shi Huangdi's domination? Luckily for the wall workers who were still alive, the end was in sight.

The Legend of Meng Jiangnu

Qin Shi Huangdi was not a popular emperor. His strict policies for controlling China created much unhappiness among the Chinese people. The following story is a legend, but like most legends, it reflects the truth.

Meng Jiangnu was a young woman who was married to an intellectual sentenced to work on the Great Wall. Because he was a frail and sickly man, Meng Jiangnu begged for him to be allowed to remain with her, but Qin Shi Huangdi's soldiers dragged him away.

That was in the spring. By autumn he had not returned, and Meng Jiangnu became very worried. She decided to make him a set of warm clothes. One night her husband appeared in a dream, telling her that he was miserable and freezing.

Meng finished the winter clothing and took it to him herself. When she arrived at the place her husband was working, she discovered that he had died and was buried in the wall. Meng Jiangnu threw herself on the wall and began sobbing. As her tears flowed, there was a mighty thunderclap, the wall split open, and the bones of her husband tumbled out. Still weeping, she gathered them up and began walking back home to give him a proper burial.

The emperor passed Meng Jiangnu on the road. Taken by her beauty, he invited her to become one of his wives. When she refused, he demanded that she marry him or be executed. Meng Jiangnu pleaded persuasively, and Qin Shi Huangdi relented. He gave her one hundred days to consider his offer but demanded that she come to his court and make him an embroidered coat during that time. He even promised her that if, after one hundred days, she did not want to become his wife, she would be free to return home and bury her husband.

Having no choice, Meng Jiangnu went to Qin Shi Huangdi's court and made the coat for him. But the emperor again demanded that she marry him. Meng Jiangnu cried that she must bury her beloved husband. She pleaded with the emperor to give her husband a formal funeral and promised to marry him afterward.

Meng Jiangnu chose a cliff overlooking the sea as the site for the funeral and burial. Qin Shi Huangdi and all of his court were in attendance. As soon as the ceremony was done, Meng Jiangnu rushed to the edge of the cliff and hurled herself into the sea. She would rather die than marry the emperor.

Chapter Four
THE SLEEPING DRAGON

(221 B.C.–210 B.C.)

QIN SHI HUANGDI'S REIGN didn't last very long—only eleven years. But even so, his head military commander, General Meng Tien, managed to get more than 1,500 miles (2,414 km) of the Great Wall built in just seven of those years. Future emperors would add another 1,600 miles (2,575 km) over the next eighteen hundred years.

The design and layout of the wall was so efficient and beautiful, it was followed by all future Chinese emperors. Whenever they built additional sections of the wall or repaired existing ones, they might expand or embellish the original design, but the basic structure was always the same—the one that Qin Shi Huangdi's architects had established.

Qin Shi Huangdi's wall was so grand and beautifully designed, later wall builders followed his plan.

A BEAUTIFUL DESIGN

The early Chinese recorded a lot of information, but they didn't record the name of the original architect. Earlier engineers had figured out how to pound dirt into a hang-tu wall and how to turn it into a tall, thick wall. But the Great Wall was different from other hang-tu walls.

The Great Wall was not only longer than any previous Chinese wall, it was also grander. Other walls had been primarily just walls. The Great Wall is a series of towers linked together by sections of wall with a roadway on top.

The Chinese still believed that China was the center of the universe, and the wall needed to reflect that. It needed to be impressive and intimidating. When the Great Wall was first built, the northern tribes wouldn't even graze their ponies within 10 miles (16 km) of it. Nobody wanted to tangle with a nation that could build such a magnificent structure.

Although the wall was built to serve a useful purpose, it was also designed to be beautiful. It might seem odd to think of a wall as beautiful, but the Great Wall was beautiful. A great deal of its beauty came from the way it unfolded across the Chinese landscape.

FENG SHUI AND THE GREAT WALL

Feng shui is the Chinese belief that there are veins running beneath the soil of the earth. All of the earth's wind and water pass through these veins, and their movements affect the course of world events—for better or worse.

The Great Wall was built according to the principles of feng shui. That's one reason it follows such a snaking path. The wall wasn't just following the geographical contours of the land. The architects (and General Meng Tien, in particular) were making sure that the wall didn't cut through any of the feng shui veins in the earth. Should a vein be cut, terrible calamities would happen. Many natural events, such as earthquakes and floods, were attributed to cuts in the earth's veins.

WHERE SHOULD THE WALL GO?

Qin Shi Huangdi's wall protected China from the northern barbarians, so it was built along China's northern border from east to west. It snaked over mountains, down into valleys, and skirted rivers and sheer cliffs. It curved north, then turned back south—often several times in a single mile. The only time it ran in a straight line, or at least something that resembled a straight line, was when it crossed the desert.

Because of this serpentine design, the Great Wall has been compared to a sleeping dragon—a sleeping dragon guarding China. In China, the dragon is a great, mythical creature full of power and a symbol of good luck. As the Great Wall creeps across China, it looks like a giant dragon stretched out in sleep along the top of the mountains.

As other emperors expanded and rebuilt the wall, they also embellished the design so that the Great Wall we see (most of which was constructed or rebuilt by the Ming dynasty during the 1300s and 1400s) is a truly beautiful piece of architecture. But no amount of brick or embellishment would have made the Great Wall beautiful if the original design hadn't been so grandly simple.

A DIVIDING LINE

Qin Shi Huangdi wanted the wall to separate the settled Chinese from the nomadic northern tribes. Fertile farmland was supposed to be on the southern, or Chinese, side of the wall, and nomadic grazing lands were to be on the outside, or northern, side of the wall. Though it was built to keep the groups apart, it didn't work out quite that way.

In some regions, there wasn't a clear-cut division between the two landscapes. In order to follow the curves of the terrain, sometimes the wall sliced farmland in half. Other times it enclosed arid grazing land.

Because of this, although the Great Wall was usually able to keep out invaders, it wasn't able to keep the Chinese entirely contained. Farmers on the Chinese side saw fertile farmlands outside the wall. They moved to the other side and began farming. Then they made friends with nomadic tribes and began trading with them. So right from the start, no matter where the wall was built, there was always some intermingling of the people on either side of it.

TOWERS FIRST

Historians aren't sure, but they believe that construction of the wall started in the mountains of eastern China and moved westward into the Gobi Desert. First built were the towers.

In Qin Shi Huangdi's time, the towers were usually constructed from wood and sun-baked brick. If wood was not available in the region, it was hauled in by supply cart. Bricks were made by mixing water with whatever dirt was at hand. The resulting mud was packed into wooden molds and set out in the sun to dry. After the mud bricks had dried, the molds were removed and used again.

Each tower was about 40 feet (12 m) square at the base, tapering to about 30 feet (9 m) square at the top. Each was about 40 feet (12 m) high.

The towers were spaced about two bow-shot lengths apart, along the entire length of the Great Wall. This spacing guaranteed that any enemy caught between the towers could be shot by an archer.

Towers were placed about two bow-shot lengths apart along the wall.

LIFE IN A TOWER

A tower usually had three levels connected by ladders. Many towers even had rooms, with doors that could be closed for privacy.

Crossbows, a Chinese invention, hung on the walls. Armor and helmets were neatly stacked, and grease and other maintenance supplies were kept handy. Jars of drinking water lined the walls. Most towers also had some sort of grill for cooking. During times of unrest or battle, the soldiers manned the towers around the clock.

A platform at the top of the tower could be reached by an inside ladder. The platform was surrounded by a crenellated parapet, a low stone wall with viewing areas cut into it. The parapet kept the soldiers from falling off and protected them from enemy arrows. There were crenellated sections of the wall, too, that had slits in them for shooting at the enemy. By the time the entire Great Wall was completed—a project that took almost two thousand years—more than twenty-five thousand towers had been built.

SOLDIERS AND THE GREAT WALL

Chinese soldiers were excellent warriors, trained in hand-to-hand combat. Most soldiers carried iron knives and swords and wore leather helmets and tunics. Some of the soldiers were trained to shoot crossbows, while others were trained to fight with swords on horseback.

Some soldiers served as scouts. Sand was often spread out on the ground on the northern side of the wall, and every morning scouts would search the sand for signs of footprints. Often they ventured some distance north of the wall to make sure that the enemy wasn't creeping up. Guard dogs usually accompanied the scouts wherever they went and were kept on the wall itself, to bark out a warning if anyone approached.

CONNECTING THE TOWERS

Once the towers were built, the next step was to connect them with a section of wall. Towers were built from brick, but when it came to the wall, workers usually used whatever was on hand. The hang-tu method was certainly versatile. Once a mold was built, almost anything could go into it. Rocks, dirt, twigs, and sand—they all went into the Great Wall. If the layers were thin enough, or if some water was added, almost anything could be compacted into a wall.

The wall was built wide enough for four horses to travel side by side along the top. All sections of the

wall are between 15 and 25 feet (4.6 and 7.6 m) thick at the base and about 13 feet (4 m) wide at the top.

Workers on the Great Wall had no heavy building equipment. They carried earth in baskets and pounded it firm with simple hand tools.

OUTPOSTS ON THE OTHER SIDE

Qin Shi Huangdi didn't want to take any chances that China would be invaded. He valued his throne so much that a thick wall, 3,000 miles (4,828 km) long, with soldiers in watchtowers, wasn't quite enough.

To make doubly sure that any approaching invader would be seen and stopped, the defensive system of the Great Wall also included outposts, separate from the wall, built on the northern side of it. These outposts were large towers that were constructed anyplace an enemy might breach the wall, such as valley openings or mountain passes.

Each outpost housed several hundred soldiers. Because outposts were the first line of defense, they were designed to be self-sufficient. Each was stocked with enough supplies to withstand a siege of four months. More than fifteen thousand early warning outposts were built along the northern side of the Great Wall.

"CALLING ALL TOWERS"

The early warning outposts and lookout towers ensured that any approaching enemies would be seen. But what happened when enemy troops were actually spotted?

Each tower along the wall was built within sight of the next one. The towers communicated with each other through smoke signals during the day and bonfires at night. To ensure that the smoke was thick, black, and visible, the tower sentries burned a mixture of wood, straw, and wolf dung. Smoke coming from a tower indicated that the wall near it was under attack. Each tower passed on the message, which was carried along the wall—tower by tower.

There was an organized code for the signals. One column of smoke meant that one hundred enemy troops were attacking, two columns meant five hundred, three columns of smoke meant one thousand enemies, and four columns meant five thousand troops were attacking. Five columns of smoke meant real trouble. Five beacon fires meant that more than ten thousand enemy troops were attacking the wall.

Soldiers raced to the attack from other parts of the wall, traveling on horseback or on foot. The number

Above: Clay warriors found in Qin Shi Huangdi's tomb are replicas of real warriors who protected China and the Great Wall. *Below:* Beacon fires at the watchtowers warn soldiers stationed nearby of attack.

of soldiers ordered into battle depended on how many enemy troops the signals reported.

THE END OF THE FIRST GREAT WALL

In less than eleven years, Qin Shi Huangdi managed to force the building of nearly 3,000 miles (4,828 km) of wall across China's northern border. But everything had been sacrificed to its construction. Families had been torn apart, one million people had died, and the entire population (what was left of it) was in poverty.

Qin Shi Huangdi had become the First Sovereign Emperor of China, but he had done so at great cost. Because he became the first emperor through bullying, deceit, and conquest, he never had the wholehearted backing of the Chinese people. In building the Great Wall, Qin Shi Huangdi managed to anger everyone. By 210 B.C., the Chinese people were exhausted and bankrupt as well.

Qin Shi Hunagdi's Great Wall followed China's northern border for 3,000 miles (4,828 km).

The Great Wall of Qin Shi Huangdi, 221 B.C.–210 B.C.

Qin Wall

Miles
0   200   400
0   200 400 600
Kilometers

N

ASIA

Huang R.

Jiangxi R.

current border of China

Zhu R.

YELLOW SEA

EAST CHINA SEA

PACIFIC OCEAN

SOUTH CHINA SEA

Chapter Five
PROSPERITY AND THE SILK ROAD

(210 B.C.–A.D. 300)

QIN SHI HUANGDI'S REIGN lasted only eleven years. It must have seemed an eternity to the Chinese people. Those lucky enough to escape working on the wall still had to pay enormous taxes. The tax monies went directly to the emperor to help pay for the wall, as well as his palaces, his tomb, and his opulent lifestyle.

WHO WILL BE THE NEXT EMPEROR?

Qin Shi Huangdi died in 210 B.C., while visiting Hebei on the coast. No one knows if he died from natural causes or was murdered. Either way, his death was sudden and unexpected. Although he had a son and legitimate heir to his throne, Prince Fu Su, the Qin dynasty crumbled almost immediately.

At the time of the emperor's death, General Meng Tien and Prince Fu Su were in the north, supervising the

Above: A mural from A.D. 200 to 400 shows a camel and merchant on the Silk Road. *Right:* Modern camel caravans still travel the route of the Silk Road to China.

building of the Great Wall—and fighting off the Xiongnu, the most troublesome northern nomads. But two other advisers—Li Si and Zhao Gao—were with Qin Shi Huangdi at the time of his death, and within hours, they decided that they should control China.

But first they had to get rid of both Prince Fu Su and General Meng Tien. Meng Tien was an old family friend of the Qin family. If Prince Fu Su became emperor, he would turn to General Meng Tien for advice—not to Li Si or Zhao Gao. And if they just got rid of Prince Fu Su, General Meng Tien was sure to protest and rally the soldiers.

Li Si and Zhao Gao decided to keep the emperor's death a secret, at least until they could get the body out of Hebei and back to the palace. The journey took weeks. To disguise the smell of the emperor's decomposing body, they placed it in a carriage covered with a load of dead fish. By the time they reached the palace, they had worked out a plan.

THE END OF THE QIN DYNASTY

To get rid of both Prince Fu Su and General Meng Tien, Li Si and Zhao Gao sent forged letters to both men. The letters said, "As to Fu Su, who, never having done anything worthy of merit himself, yet dares to complain and speak ill of all I do; and as to Meng Tien, who has not been able to correct my son's fault during this past year: I permit both to take their own lives." They signed both letters with the emperor's name.

CLAY SOLDIERS . . . MARCHING FOREVER

Qin Shi Huangdi's opulent lifestyle wasn't just confined to his time as emperor. It even extended into the afterlife.

In 1974 while plowing a field, some Chinese peasants accidentally unearthed an extraordinary treasure: the 2,200-year-old tomb of Qin Shi Huangdi. The tomb is in an enormous 3-acre (1.2-hectare) underground vault, covered by a wooden roof and buried under several feet of earth.

The tomb was designed as a miniature replica of the kingdom of Qin. There are scaled-down cities and tiny rivers full of liquid mercury, which flow into a miniature ocean. There are even tiny palaces and pavilions. The wooden ceiling of the vault was encrusted with jewels to mimic the stars.

Inside the tomb, standing guard over all of it, is an army of seven thousand life-sized clay soldiers, complete with chariots and weapons. Given Qin Shi Huangdi's cruelty and insensitivity, the clay soldiers are an unusual break with tradition—previous Chinese kings were known for burying soldiers alive to guard their tombs.

Qin Shi Huangdi started work on his tomb as soon as he became the king of Qin, in 246 B.C., before he became emperor of all China. It took 700,000 workers

thirty-four years to complete the tomb. Archaeologists have not yet found the actual burial place of Qin Shi Huangdi himself, but historical records indicate that it was even more extravagant. They also don't expect to find the burial place intact, since later records indicate that it was broken into and robbed only four years after Qin Shi Huangdi's death.

Prince Fu Su and General Meng Tien receive the forged letters from the emperor that order them to commit suicide.

Neither Prince Fu Su, nor General Meng Tien had much choice. Tradition demanded that they commit suicide. Prince Fu Su did commit suicide, effectively ending the Qin dynasty. But General Meng Tien thought the letter was very suspicious, so he sent a messenger back to the palace to get an actual confirmation of the order.

Li Si and Zhao Gao had the messenger thrown into prison. When he didn't return, Meng Tien left the Great Wall and journeyed to the palace. As soon as he arrived, Li Si and Zhao Gao had him imprisoned, too, and sentenced him to die. Meng Tien protested his innocence, but in the end, he too committed suicide.

Once the death of Qin Shi Huangdi became public, rebellions broke out all over China. Over the next four years, these rebellions weakened even more what little was left of the Qin dynasty. Li Si and Zhao Gao were both executed.

The rebellion that finally destroyed the government was started by a soldier who was late in delivering a group of new military recruits. It had been raining hard and the roads were muddy and impassable. The soldier knew they'd all be executed for arriving late. (Qin Shi Huangdi was dead, but his policies weren't.) So instead of accepting that fate, they rebelled, and they convinced peasants from the surrounding villages to rebel with them. Local officials knew that *they'd* be executed just for reporting the uprising, so they kept quiet. By the time the central government found out about the rebellion, it had grown too large to contain.

By 206 B.C., only four years after Qin Shi Huangdi's death, his repressive government and the forced building of the Great Wall were no more.

A NEW DYNASTY

A group of people from the Han region assumed control of China in 206 B.C. and founded the Han dynasty. Han emperors ruled China for the next 426 years.

At first the Han emperors focused on restoring peace and prosperity to China. Arts, literature, and intellectual freedom flourished during the Han dynasty. Many inventions we consider to be uniquely Chinese were developed during these four hundred years.

In the decades after Qin Shi Huangdi's death, the Great Wall fell into disrepair. The Chinese people were so disillusioned with the project that they abandoned all work on it. For the next one hundred years, few new wall sections were built, and most of the wall wasn't manned or maintained.

But the northern tribe of the Xiongnu were still a threat. By the time the sixth Han emperor, Emperor Wu Di, assumed control in 141 B.C., the

> "A beacon every 5 li, a tower every 10 li, a fort every 30 li, and a castle every 100 li."
>
> **—Emperor Wu Di**

The Xiongnu, like the invader pictured here battling a Chinese soldier, took advantage of the crumbling wall to renew their attacks.

Great Wall was crumbling, and the Xiongnu were again invading the northern Chinese states on a regular basis. Something would have to be done.

WU DI'S WALL

The next large section of the Great Wall was built between 121 B.C. and 101 B.C., during the reign of Emperor Wu Di. He hoped to subdue again the Xiongnu and establish secure trade routes with the western world.

Wu Di followed the original basic design for the wall but significantly expanded it. According to records kept by the Han, Wu Di decreed that the wall should have "a beacon every 5 li, a tower every 10 li, a fort every 30 li, and a castle every 100 li." (If you recall, a li is a Chinese measurement roughly equivalent to 1,760 feet (536 m).) He had the Great Wall lengthened in the west by 300 miles (483 km) and added a chain of watchtowers, not connected by wall sections, that stretched for 70 miles (113 km) beyond that.

Some parts of the original Han Great Wall are still standing, though most was rebuilt during the Ming dynasty.

Wu Di's wall (as it came to be called) was built using the hang-tu method of construction. The new sections ran mostly across the western desert, where very little dirt, stone, or wood was available, So workers used sand, the branches of tamarisk (a desert shrub), and reeds. They first made a layer of reeds and tamarisk branches. Then they added a layer of sand mixed with water and tamped everything down. The resulting wall was as hard as concrete.

Workers on Wu Di's section of the Great Wall apparently found better working conditions than those during Qin Shi Huangdi's time. The wall was still built by people who were drafted (taken without their consent from the general population). No written records or folk stories indicate they suffered great hardship.

Wu Di's reign began a new way of using the Great Wall. It was still manned by soldiers and used for defensive purposes. But after waging war against the Xiongnu and conquering them, Wu Di set about establishing peaceful relations with the northern nomadic tribes. Peace along the Great Wall secured the way for a flourishing trade route to the rest of the world.

THE SILK ROAD

The Han dynasty was known for its openness toward other countries. This stood in great contrast to Qin Shi Huangdi and the Qin dynasty, which was determined to close China off from the outside world.

China continued to have a more advanced culture than most nations. The Chinese of this period recognized that other nations wanted what they had: silk, paper, tea, spices, jade, and other luxuries. Beginning in the reign of Wu Di, a trade route along the wall emerged that would flourish for several centuries.

The Silk Road, as this route came to be called, established itself in the shadow of the Great Wall because that was the safest place to travel. Bandits roamed the Chinese countryside, and there was still the occasional attack from northern nomadic tribes. But Wu Di made sure that the entire length of the Great Wall was manned by soldiers. These soldiers not only protected China from invasion but also protected travelers and trading caravans from attack.

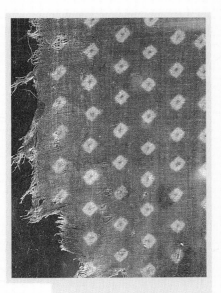

Silk from China *(as pictured above)* was desired all over the ancient world. The trade in silk gave the Silk Road its name.

LIFE ALONG THE GREAT WALL

During the Han dynasty, thousands of soldiers were positioned along the Great Wall. With peace mostly a reality, the average soldier didn't spend a lot of time fighting. Soldiers stationed on the Great Wall were a lot like modern-day police or customs officers. They made sure that local people obeyed the laws, and they checked the identification of travelers and caravans that passed through the gates.

There were many gates in this huge length of brick and earth. It was through these gates that travelers and caravans passed in and out of China. The large double-doored gates were heavily fortified and often had a second, lower wall in front of them for added protection.

Near every gate, a market town sprang up. Caravans of camels plodded through the wall on their way to the Persian Empire (what would become Iran and Turkey) with silk and tea. Other traders headed

CHINESE ACCOMPLISHMENTS

The Chinese eventually opened their country and began trading with the outside world. Other cultures were amazed at the things the Chinese had.

The Chinese were the first to produce paper, porcelain (a type of fine pottery), and to weave silk. They were experts at jade carving, producing beautiful jewelry, art objects, and even weapons from the hard green stone.

Nearly one hundred years before Columbus even thought about crossing the ocean, the Chinese were sailing as far as Africa using a compass they had created. They were also drawing detailed maps of their journeys.

The Chinese also developed the first seismograph (an instrument that detects earthquakes). This early seismograph *(below)* was an ornamental cast-bronze figure with nine dragons facing outward in a circle. Each dragon held a delicately balanced ball in its mouth and faced toward a different Chinese province. If a ball fell from a dragon's mouth, it meant that an earthquake had occurred in the province that dragon faced. Odd as it sounds, this early seismograph appears to have been an accurate earthquake indicator.

east through the wall on their way to Chinese cities, carrying loads of wool, linen, glass, and raisins—a Middle Eastern food the Chinese considered exotic. Trade along the Silk Road stretched all the way from China's eastern seacoast to areas around the Mediterranean Sea.

Soldiers who worked on the Great Wall were often stationed there indefinitely. Towers were stocked with weapons and supplies, the smoke and fire beacons were kept ready, and watches were scheduled around the clock. Most soldiers lived in houses built nearby. If soldiers were married, their families lived there with them. They planted gardens and raised domestic livestock, which provided fresh vegetables and meat for the garrisons. Being a soldier on the Great Wall was a normal, uneventful job.

THE END OF THE WALL . . . AGAIN

When Wu Di died in 87 B.C., the peace and prosperity he had established along the wall continued. Future emperors in the Han dynasty experienced all sorts of problems (including assassinations), but peaceful trade between China and other nations continued to flourish for the next two hundred years. Even the dreaded Xiongnu became valued trading partners.

But the Xiongnu weren't the only barbarian tribes in the north. By A.D. 200, other tribes had banded together and the wall was under attack again. As these attacks escalated, the Han emperors found it increasingly difficult to keep the barbarians out. China was a large country, with a large bureaucratic government. Because of its size and population, it was always a difficult country for any emperor to manage. And not all emperors were powerful and smart military leaders. For them, trying to run the country while fending off invasions was nearly impossible.

In A.D. 220, the Han dynasty collapsed. With the collapse of the Han, peaceful trade along the Silk Road disappeared. The barbarian tribes overran the wall in several places. By A.D. 300, the Great Wall was actually controlled by northern tribes. In effect, China's northern boundary had shifted southward.

The northern barbarians were no longer on the other side of the Great Wall. They were in China.

Chapter Six
MONGOLS AND THE MING
(300–1620)

BARBARIANS DIDN'T SO MUCH conquer China as infiltrate it. Rather than charging and hacking their way south, they settled in the regions around the Great Wall. They farmed and intermarried with the Chinese. Some of the barbarian leaders even married Chinese princesses. In the process, they became more Chinese than barbarian.

For the next one thousand years, various emperors and dynasties came and went in China. Some of them attempted to maintain the wall, repairing old sections and building new ones. But most felt that a defensive military strategy, such as a wall, was not a good way to defend China.

Above: Genghis Khan, a Mongol ruler, unified many of the nomadic northern tribes and conquered most of central Asia. *Right:* Mongol warriors were accomplished horsemen.

For several hundred years after the Han dynasty collapsed, China's emperors took an offensive approach to protecting the country. They didn't sit behind a wall and wait. They went out and attacked.

The wall fell into disrepair. Guard towers were abandoned, and weeds worked their way between the stones and bricks, creating hulking ruins. In many places, the wall crumbled into a heap of dirt and bricks. In other places, there were huge gaps where invaders had broken through. The Great Wall might have deteriorated into a pile of dirt were it not for the arrival of the Mongols.

GENGHIS KHAN . . . "GREATEST OF RULERS"

Although the Xiongnu barbarians had essentially become Chinese, the threat to China from the north had never completely vanished. Other nomadic people still lived north of China. As a general group, they were referred to as Mongols. They had always been a problem for China, but around 1200, they became a serious threat. At that time, a leader emerged among them who unified all the different Mongol tribes and led them into organized battles. His name was Genghis Khan.

A Mongol warrior could shoot a bow and arrow accurately from the back of a galloping horse.

Genghis Khan, whose given name was Temüjin, was born around A.D. 1160. "Genghis Khan" was an honorary title he adopted in 1206. Roughly translated, it means "Greatest of Rulers" or "Emperor of All Men."

By gathering together all the separate Mongol tribes, Genghis Khan was able to create a military force that numbered in the hundreds of thousands. The organized armies of the khan, brandishing swords and mounted on swift horses, swept over everything in their path. By 1206 Genghis Khan had managed to conquer most of central Asia.

Because so much of it was crumbling, the Great Wall was no barrier to the Mongol forces. By 1215 Genghis Khan had conquered much of China. The Mongols ruled China for about 150 years, calling themselves the Yuan dynasty.

LIVING UNDER MONGOL RULE

Genghis Khan died in 1227, but his forces kept right on going. By roughly 1250, the Mongols controlled everything from present-day Korea to present-day Turkey.

Genghis Khan's grandson became the Mongol emperor in 1260. Calling himself Kublai Khan, he made the present-day city of Beijing in northern China the seat of his government.

GENGHIS AND KUBLAI

"Khan" is an honorary title, much like "emperor" or "king." Both Genghis Khan and his grandson, Kublai Khan, adopted the title during their reigns.

The Mongols' forces were feared throughout Asia. The Chinese despised them as the conquerors of their country. But as rulers of China, both Genghis Khan and Kublai Khan were basically tolerant and did many good things. Both continued to use the existing government structure initially established by previous Chinese emperors, so life changed little for the Chinese.

Under Kublai Khan, China made more contact with the outside world than even during the Han dynasty with its Silk Road. Dignitaries came from all over Asia and the Mediterranean regions to visit his court. The ruler was open to new ideas and welcomed visitors.

One reason the Chinese hated the Mongols was because they hired non-Chinese people to work in government positions. Kublai Khan not only hired Mongols, he hired Uighurs from central Asia, Arabs, and even an Italian named Marco Polo. While it's not unusual for a conquering nation to use their own people and others to fill government positions, the Chinese still considered themselves the only people of culture and civilization and the only ones fit to run their country.

The Italian explorer Marco Polo *(handing paper to the emperor)* joined the court of Kublai Khan.

Everyday life for the Chinese didn't change much under the Yuan dynasty. The Mongols kept most of China the way it had been. This was unusual, since the Mongols typically turned any country they conquered into grazing land for their ponies.

But the Chinese people despised the Mongol rulers anyway. To them, the Mongols were foreigners, and foreigners had never been welcome in China. The Chinese wanted the Mongols out.

THE FALL OF THE MONGOL . . . AND THE RISE OF THE MING

When Kublai Khan died in 1294, the Chinese people saw their chance to regain control of their country. During the next seventy years, various Chinese rebel groups mounted surprise attacks and worked hard to undermine Mongol authority.

The Mongols were finally driven out of China by a former monk named Zhu Yuanzhang. In 1368 Zhu Yuanzhang became the first emperor of the Ming dynasty and took the name Hongwu.

KEEP THE BARBARIANS OUT!

The barbarians might again be on the other side of the Great Wall (what was left of it), but the threat of invasion still loomed. The Mongol forces wanted to get China back just as badly as the Chinese people wanted to keep them out.

> "At each signal station let the towers be built higher and stronger. . . . Be on your guard at all times with anxious care."
>
> —Hongwu

Hongwu decided to rebuild the Great Wall. Protecting Beijing, only twelve miles (19.3 km) south of the wall, became an important task of his government. The Mongol forces were always very close, and the threat of invasion was real. It was vital that the Great Wall's fortifications be strengthened and staffed with soldiers.

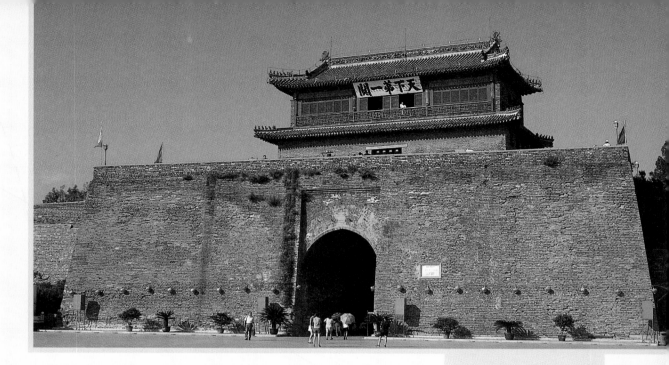

Rebuilding the Great Wall was no longer just a
quick repair job. After nearly one thousand years of
general neglect, everything built by Qin Shi Huangdi
and succeeding dynasties had deteriorated almost
beyond repair. A new Great Wall would have to be
built. Emperor Hongwu immediately issued orders
to all his generals to begin work on the Great Wall, starting with the
towers.

His direct orders were: "At each signal station let the towers be built
higher and stronger; within must be laid up food, fuel, medicine, and
weapons for four moons [approximately four months]. Beside the
tower let a wall be opened, enclosed by a wall as high as the tower
itself, presenting the appearance of a double gateway, inner and outer.
Be on your guard at all times with anxious care."

Hongwu also demanded that any gate in the wall that carts and
horsemen used was to be guarded by one hundred men. Smaller gates,
where herdsmen came and went, were to be guarded by ten men.

The towers were just the beginning. The entire Great Wall was to be
rebuilt.

A NEW GREAT WALL

When we look at the Great Wall of China, most of what we see was constructed during the Ming dynasty. Nearly everything built before that
had deteriorated by the time the Ming came to power. Starting with

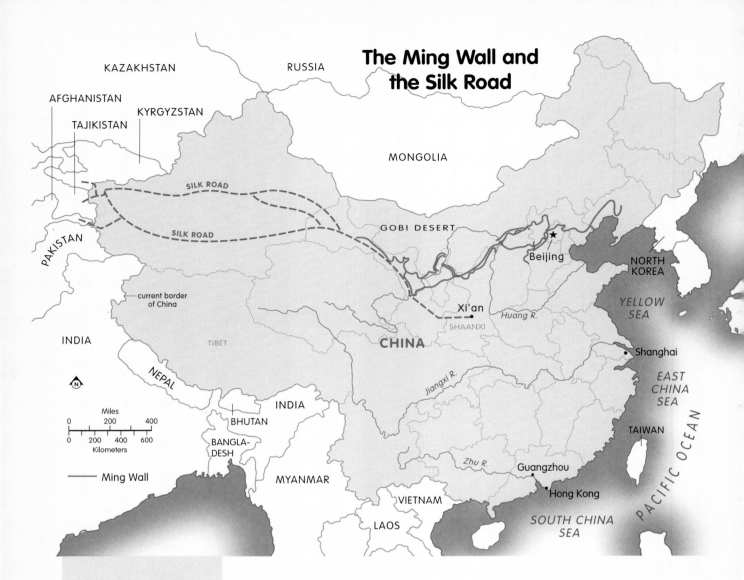

The Ming Wall and the Silk Road

KAZAKHSTAN

RUSSIA

AFGHANISTAN

KYRGYZSTAN

TAJIKISTAN

MONGOLIA

SILK ROAD

PAKISTAN

SILK ROAD

GOBI DESERT

★ Beijing

NORTH KOREA

current border of China

YELLOW SEA

INDIA

Xi'an

Huang R.

SHAANXI

CHINA

TIBET

NEPAL

Shanghai

EAST CHINA SEA

Miles
0   200   400
0 200 400 600
Kilometers

INDIA

Jiangxi R.

BHUTAN

BANGLA-DESH

TAIWAN

PACIFIC OCEAN

Ming Wall

MYANMAR

Zhu R.

Guangzhou

Hong Kong

VIETNAM

LAOS

SOUTH CHINA SEA

This map of modern China traces the trading routes known as the Silk Road. It also shows the Great Wall and its extensions in the Ming dynasty.

Hongwu, the monk-turned-emperor, succeeding Ming emperors rebuilt and expanded the Great Wall for the next 276 years. The Ming ruled China from 1368 until 1644, and the Great Wall became a continuous Ming dynasty project. By the time the Ming were through, the Great Wall stretched for more than 4,000 miles (6,437 km).

Much of the new Great Wall, built during the Ming dynasty, is actually a little bit south of the Great Wall constructed from the Qin through Han dynasties. So little remained of the Qin and Han dynasties' walls, many people assumed that the Great Wall didn't exist before the Ming. As the Great

Wall wound across China's northern border, the Ming incorporated the earlier constructions where they could, but more often they had to build an entirely new wall.

Each Ming emperor rebuilt and extended the wall. The last powerful Ming emperor, Wanli, did so much wall building that some in future generations assumed that the entire wall had been built by him. Wanli ruled China from 1572 until his death in 1620. It was Wanli, along with Hong Zhi, a Ming emperor before him, who created the magnificent towers, gates, and mighty stone walls we still see.

Emperor Wanli was the foremost builder of the Ming Great Wall.

GATES, TOWERS, AND WALLS

The three main components of the Ming Great Wall are gates, towers, and walls. All had existed in previous walls, but the Ming builders refined them and made them more uniform.

The strongest fortifications were built at gates in the wall. The largest gates, where troops passed through, were built at places of military importance. Because these openings were large, they should have been the easiest places to attack. The Ming fortified each gate so heavily, though, that they were usually the most difficult places for any enemy to try to break through.

Signal towers went by many names: beacons, beacon terraces, kiosks, or smoke mounds. As in the past, the lower part of a tower was used for storage and housing, the upper part for lookouts and signaling.

Walls linked the towers. Ming builders followed the basic wall plan developed by Qin Shi Huangdi. The walls were about 21 feet (6.4 m) thick at the base, tapering to 19 feet (5.8 m) at the top. In most places, they were about 26 feet (7.9 m) tall. But unlike the Qin and Han dynasties' walls, the Ming wall was completely covered in brick or stone.

This is the highest watch-tower of the Ming Great Wall. It was constructed near Beijing to protect the city.

A UNIFORM GREAT WALL

The Ming Great Wall was still built using the hang-tu method. However, the layers of earth were thicker—usually about 8 inches (20 cm), instead of 3 or 4 inches (7 to 10 cm).

The methods might have been the same, but the Great Wall of the Ming dynasty was much grander. And it was more uniform. The Ming builders didn't just settle for whatever materials were available. When lumber was needed, crews traveled to the closest forest, no matter how far away. In the same way, quarried stone might be hauled great distances for use on the wall.

EASIER BUILDING METHODS

Hundreds of thousands of men were enlisted to rebuild the Great Wall. During the Ming dynasty, workers usually had adequate food, clothing, and housing. They also had better tools than Qin and Han dynasty workers. But it was still long, hard work.

Workers on previous walls had sweated and toiled miserably to get dirt and bricks up to the top of the wall. Ming workers still used woven baskets for hauling dirt, but they also used wheelbarrows and a rope and pulley system to get dirt and rocks in place.

Workers on the Ming wall used a pulley system *(above)* to transport dirt to the top of the construction site and wheelbarrows *(below)* to haul building supplies.

Still, human hands were the basic tools. In areas where the land was hilly and steep, workers would form a line, often miles long, and pass materials from one person to the next until they reached their destination.

Bricks baked in kilns (ovens) formed the exterior of the Ming dynasty's Great Wall. In most sections, the Ming used brick walls rather than wooden planks for the hang-tu mold. And unlike the earlier constructions, these brick hang-tu molds weren't removed but remained in place to become part of the wall.

But in other aspects, the wall was the same as previous ones. The Ming filled the space between the two brick walls with crushed rocks, dirt layers, and a muddy mixture that hardened as it dried. In those sections where the wall was entirely dirt, it was still covered with bricks.

In many places, particularly around Beijing, the base of the Ming Great Wall was built of quarried stone. Stone, sturdier than brick, was used to construct the passes too. By the 1500s, quarrying techniques had been refined, making the stone easier to cut and transport.

KILNS AND BRICK MAKING

The Ming were experts at brick making. They developed and refined the technique of using high-temperature kilns to bake bricks to rock hardness. Modern bricks are made by this method.

To build the Ming wall, kilns were constructed next to the Great Wall and the bricks were made right there. Although stone and wood were delivered to sites that didn't have them locally, clay was seldom delivered—it was too hard to keep it damp and soft on a long journey. If clay wasn't locally available, dirt mixed with water was used for the bricks. To make sure the bricks were all the same size, workers packed the brick material into wooden molds. When it had hardened enough to be handled, the molds were removed and the bricks were baked in a kiln.

Ming kilns were made of stone and shaped like a beehive. A fire was built inside the structure, the smoke escaping through a small hole at the top. The soft bricks were then placed inside the kiln and baked for hours. When the fire went out and the kiln had cooled, the bricks were removed for use on the wall. There would be many kilns operating on any section of the Ming wall, and hundreds of workers making bricks.

In China's northern mountainous region, the government established several quarries (places where stone could be removed from the earth). Stone cutting was a skilled job, assigned to special workers. Using metal chisels and hammers, workers chipped away until they had a block of the required size. It was loaded onto a cart, using rollers and pulleys, and delivered to the site. Because granite, an extremely strong rock, was used for the base, the Ming Great Wall was stronger than other hang-tu walls—which meant that it was capable of carrying more weight.

These new construction methods made the wall sturdier and a little easier to rebuild. But it also meant that skilled workers were needed. Peasants and intellectuals were fine for building Qin Shi Huangdi's wall. Hauling buckets of dirt doesn't require any particular training. But producing evenly shaped bricks in a kiln and cutting chunks of granite into precise stone blocks requires skill.

A BEAUTIFUL WALL

Historians know that every Chinese dynasty that worked on the Great Wall used the same design (a series of towers, linked by sections of wall) and the same construction method (hang-tu, or pounded and compressed layers). But the Ming dynasty took the construction method and basic design and created a more beautiful structure.

The Great Wall of the Ming dynasty was faced with cut stone or brick. This historic illustration shows bricklayers at work.

Ming Wall

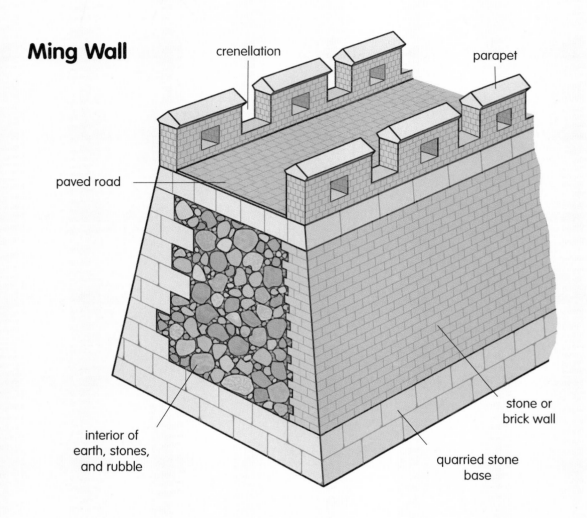

crenellation

parapet

paved road

interior of
earth, stones,
and rubble

stone or
brick wall

quarried stone
base

This early map of a
section of the Ming
Great Wall depicts an
area about 30 miles (50
km) from the eastern
end. It shows
watchtowers, gates, and
buildings for the military.
Mountains and tents of
the nomads beyond
them are at the top.

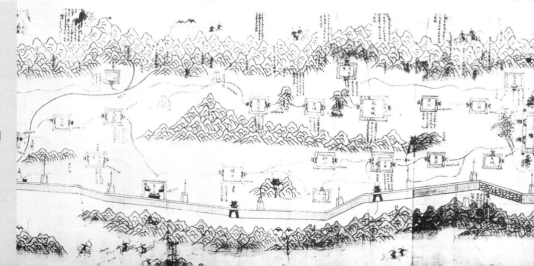

In addition to skilled bricklayers and stonecutters, historians know that architects were employed on the Ming Great Wall because many of the towers and gates resemble ornate temples and official buildings. Ming architects clearly felt that the wall should be beautiful as well as practical.

In addition to the actual towers, forts, and gates at the passes, the wall itself shows the influence of architects. The bricks of the facing were of the highest quality and were laid in perfect patterns. Skilled bricklayers might have done this, but historians believe it more likely that architects created the designs.

The Ming wall was built with drains in it, another sign of architectural engineering. Whenever it rained, the rainwater drained off to the north, or Mongol, side of the wall. Previous walls had not had drains, which had contributed to their deterioration. Water worked its way between the bricks and when winter came, the water froze, expanded, and cracked the bricks and mortar. Without drains, the Ming Great Wall wouldn't be standing either. Like the previous walls, it would have broken down into a heap of rubble.

BETTER SIGNALS

Another thing the Ming changed when they rebuilt the Great Wall was the signaling system. In the 1,500 years since the Qin dynasty wall had been built, rockets and gunpowder had been invented. The signaling code was still the same, but rockets were used along with the smoke beacons.

The Ming Great Wall was rarely breached because throughout the dynasty it was manned by more than one million soldiers. Having driven the Mongols to the other side of the wall, the Ming emperors were not about to let them back in.

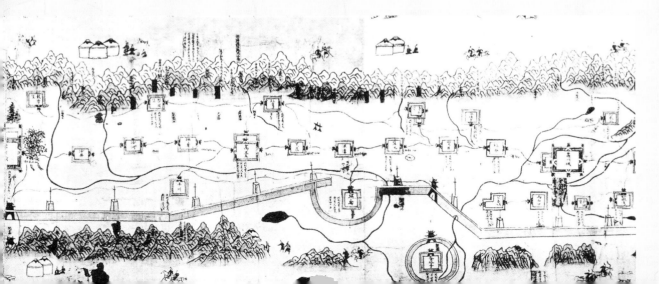

Chapter Seven
INTO THE FUTURE WITH WANLI'S WALL

(1620–present)

WANLI WAS THE LAST EMperor to work on the Great Wall of China. He extended the wall to its greatest lengths and fortified it more than any other emperor. Yet Wanli also started the Great Wall on its decline.

THE DECLINE OF THE MING DYNASTY

Wanli, the thirteenth Ming emperor, was the last powerful emperor of the Ming dynasty. During Wanli's rule, China enjoyed peace and military security, It also traded with most of Europe. All three of these things—peace, security, and trade—were possible because of the Great Wall. When the Ming dynasty—and the Great Wall—declined, so did peace and prosperity.

Wanli came to power in 1572 and did most of his wall building during the first twenty years of

Above: Zhang Zhu Zheng was Wanli's trusted friend and adviser. He was responsible for much of the rebuilding of the Ming Great Wall. *Right:* This section of the Ming wall hasn't yet been restored.

his reign. He started off by completing projects begun by Emperor Hongwu and continued to expand and fortify the Great Wall. In short, he was acting the way all Ming emperors before him did: Build more wall, add more soldiers.

Then, sometime around 1590, Wanli's friend and most trusted adviser, Zhang Zhu Zheng, died. Not until his death did it become apparent just how heavily Wanli had relied upon his adviser's judgment and just how instrumental Zhang Zhu Zheng had been in rebuilding the Great Wall and running China. Without Zhang Zhu Zheng, Wanli turned out to be a terrible ruler.

He began to act very oddly. He lost all interest in governing China, let alone expanding or maintaining the Great Wall. He secluded himself inside his palace and refused to meet with any of his advisers. He grew fearful of comets, eclipses, sudden floods, and droughts. He also became wildly extravagant, spending more than nine million ounces of silver on building royal palaces. He spent even more than that on gifts for his friends and relatives.

By 1599 Wanli had spent so much money, China was on the verge of economic collapse. Canal and farming projects were abandoned, and the construction of official buildings came to a halt. Soldiers and government workers weren't paid, so they drifted away from their jobs. China's whole government structure fell apart.

The construction of the Great Wall also suffered. There was no money to pay soldiers to guard the wall or to pay for needed repairs and expansion.

By the time Wanli died in 1620, China was in a disastrous mess. For more than twenty years, he had refused to govern China and had spent the money collected in taxes on himself. Because he was the emperor, no one dared question his right to do this. If he had stepped aside and let someone else govern, China might have been better off. But, although he had no interest in running the government himself, he didn't name a successor. Consequently, all of China suffered.

RELIGION, NOT WALLS

Three more Ming emperors followed Wanli, but none were strong rulers, and none were able to reverse China's decline. Perhaps more importantly, none of them had any money to expand and fortify the Great Wall. Brick by brick, the wall crumbled. Because it was no longer staffed with soldiers, northern tribes overran parts of it. In 1644 another northern group, the Manchu, broke through the wall and took control of China.

The Manchu also founded their own dynasty: the Qing dynasty. The Qing ruled China from 1644 until 1911.

The Qing, the northern Manchu who ruled China for more than 250 years, held court at Beijing.

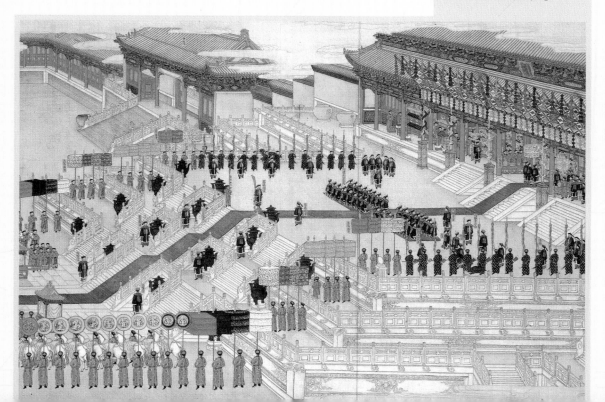

THE BOXER REBELLION AND THE GREAT WALL

In 1899, when four newspaper reporters in Denver, Colorado, needed to come up with a story, they invented one about the Great Wall. Their headline in the next day's papers read, "Great Wall Doomed!" The reporters claimed that a group of Chinese engineers was traveling in the United States, consulting with other engineers on how to demolish the Great Wall. China wanted to tear down the wall to demonstrate to the world that it wished for more open relations.

The story was completely false, but other newspapers picked it up and published it. When the story reached China, the Chinese newspapers reported that American and European soldiers were on their way to China to take down the Great Wall by force.

The Chinese people were outraged. Rebellion had been simmering for a year, and resentment against foreigners in China was strong. This particular story was the last straw. Riots broke out across the country, and foreign embassies were attacked.

During what was known as the Boxer Rebellion, other countries sent forces into China to protect their embassies and their citizens living there. Thousands of Chinese were killed. Many historians have blamed the false newspaper story about the Great Wall for the increasing Chinese attacks against foreigners *(above)* during the Boxer Rebellion.

The Manchu, like the earlier northern tribes that had overrun the wall and infiltrated China, became almost more Chinese than the native Chinese people.

The Manchu never felt any need to rebuild the Great Wall to keep out other northern tribes. They adopted a completely new policy. The emperors of the Qing dynasty managed to bring the leaders of Tibet, Mongolia, and other northern areas under control by religious and political pressure.

This policy worked so well that no emperor after the Ming paid any attention to the Great Wall as a means of defense. Until the 1960s, no ruler paid any attention at all to the Great Wall.

TEAR DOWN THE GREAT WALL

In 1911 a revolution intent on social reform ousted the Manchu and later established the Republic of China. Ten years later, the Chinese Communist Party was founded—the party that dominates the government of modern China. As the Chinese people struggled to form a new identity, the Great Wall was virtually forgotten.

The citizens of the city of Hankou fled before the soldiers of Mao Zedong. Mao founded the Chinese Communist Party, which has governed modern China since 1949.

Under the Communists, China again closed its doors to the rest of the world. The new rulers of China had no use for the Great Wall. It certainly wasn't part of any military defense strategy. And with foreigners banned from the country, the wall wasn't even a tourist attraction.

In the 1960s, the Great Wall finally came under scrutiny by the Chinese government—to its detriment. A forced Cultural Revolution was taking place in China. China's political, cultural, and intellectual traditions were decreed to be worthless, old-fashioned, even hateful, and, therefore, had to be eliminated.

For the next few years, it was almost as if Qin Shi Huangdi was again the emperor. A massive campaign to destroy thousands of priceless works of art, ancient literature, and other historical objects took place all over China. Rare books were burned, and ancient bronze statues were melted down for scrap.

The Great Wall had just barely withstood one thousand years of neglect, but it could not withstand a direct assault from a government determined to erase all ties to the past. The Chinese government used dynamite, heavy digging equipment, and other means to destroy hundreds of miles of wall.

This section of the Ming dynasty wall was damaged during the Cultural Revolution.

PRESIDENT NIXON AND THE GREAT WALL

In 1972 President Richard M. Nixon *(below, pointing)* became the first American president to visit China. His visit came at a time when China had allowed almost no foreigners into the country for more than twenty years. It was at the height of the Cultural Revolution, a time when China's Communist leaders were encouraging—even forcing—people to do away with the past, and several hundred miles of the Great Wall had been demolished.

Yet the day after Nixon arrived in China, he was taken to visit the Great Wall by Chairman Mao Zedong, the head of the Chinese Communist Party. Chairman Mao *(below left)* repeated to President Nixon an old Chinese saying: "You're not a man until you've climbed to the top."

THE RESTORATION OF THE GREAT WALL

Had this campaign of destruction continued, it's likely that the Great Wall would no longer exist. But in 1984, a new leader, Deng Xiaoping, abruptly reversed the trend of destruction when he publicly announced, "Let us love our country and restore our Great Wall."

Almost overnight the Chinese government launched a new campaign. This time the campaign was to rebuild the wall. Hundreds of miles of wall were restored. Every year more sections of the Great Wall are rescued.

Chinese workers have restored long stretches of the Great Wall.

THE GREAT WALL TODAY

Built to save China, the Great Wall no longer has any military importance—the development of missiles and satellite technology saw to that. But in 1972, China reversed its policy of isolation and opened its doors again to the rest of the world. Since the mid-1980s, the Great Wall has been China's main tourist attraction, generating millions of dollars of revenue for China every year. The Chinese people have shown a renewed sense of pride in this amazing structure built by their ancestors.

The Great Wall reflects the history of China in its bricks and dirt. It tells the stories of emperors and dynasties, of triumphs and defeat, of treachery and death. The Great Wall has been the means for both the closing and the opening of China to trade and contact with the outside world. Truly one of the greatest feats of building, the Great Wall illustrates for the world the long saga of one of the largest and oldest nations on earth.

> "Let us love our country and restore our Great Wall."
> —**Deng Xiaoping**

A Timeline of the Great Wall

4000 B.C.   Early people in China develop agriculture, which results in their settling in villages, often surrounded by protective earthen walls.

1500 B.C.   The earliest Chinese cities are built and fortified with protective walls.

475 B.C.–221 B.C.   Warring States Period, during which China is a collection of hostile separate kingdoms

221 B.C.–210 B.C.   Reign of China's first emperor, Qin Shi Huangdi. The first Great Wall is built under General Meng Tien's command.

206 B.C.   Beginning of the reign of the Han dynasty

121–101 B.C.   Han emperor Wu Di extends the Great Wall into western desert to protect trade along the Silk Road and to subdue the Xiongnu.

A.D. 220   End of the Han dynasty

A.D. 1200s   Mongol leader Genghis Khan breaks through neglected Great Wall; conquers China in 1215.

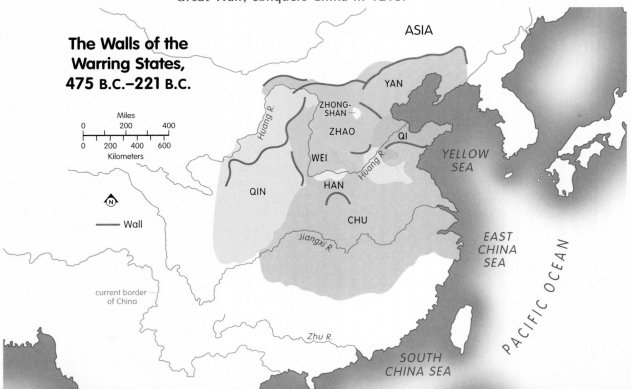

The Walls of the Warring States, 475 B.C.–221 B.C.

1260   Kublai Khan becomes Mongol emperor of China and nearby areas.

1368   Rebellion led by Zhu Yuanzhang, the first Ming emperor, ends Mongol occupation of China.

1368–1644   Rule of the Ming dynasty, when the Great Wall is rebuilt

1572–1620   Rule of Ming emperor Wanli, the period when the Great Wall took its present form

1644   The Manchu conquer China.

1644–1911   The Manchu rule China, and the Great Wall ceases to serve as a defensive border.

1949   Communists led by Mao Zedong come to power.

1960s   During the Cultural Revolution, artifacts are destroyed, including parts of the Great Wall.

1972   President Nixon visits the Great Wall.

1984   Deng Xiaoping orders restoration of the Great Wall.

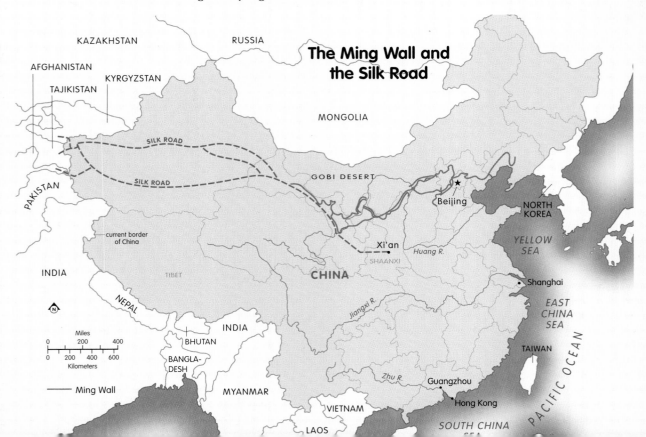

Source Notes

43   Robert Silverberg. *The Great Wall of China.* (Philadelphia: Chilton Books, 1965), 59.

46, 47   "Great Wall of China; History of Construction; The Han through Yuan Dynasties," *Encyclopedia Britannica,* n.d., <www.britannica.com> (June 2002).

56, 57   Tim McNeese, *The Great Wall of China* (San Diego, CA: Lucent, 1997), 61.

72   "Nixon's China Game," *The American Experience,* n.d., <www.pbs.org/whatson/press/winspring/amexnixonchina.html> (June 2002).

72, 73   McNeese, 85.

Selected Bibliography

Barrett, G. W. *Ancient China.* Essex, England: Longman Group Limited, 1969.

Benson, D. S. *Six Emperors: Mongolian Aggression in the Thirteenth Century.* Ashland, OH: BookMasters, Inc., 1995.

Chan, Albert. *The Glory and Fall of the Ming Dynasty.* Norman, OK: University of Oklahoma Press, 1982.

Fryer, Jonathan. *The Great Wall of China.* South Brunswick and New York: A. S. Barnes and Company, 1975.

Lai Po Kan. *The Ancient Chinese.* London: Macdonald Educational, 1980.

Li Han Hsu Tzu-kuang. *Meng Ch'iu: Famous Episodes from Chinese History and Legend.* Tokyo: Kodansha International Ltd., 1979.

Luo Zewen, Dai Wenbao, Dick Wilson, J. P. Dredge, and H. Delahaye. *The Great Wall.* New York: McGraw-Hill, 1981.

Schwartz, Daniel. *The Great Wall of China.* London: Thames and Hudson Ltd., 1990.

Silverberg, Robert. *The Great Wall of China.* Philadelphia: Chilton Books, 1965.

Strathern, Paul. *The Silk and Spice Routes: Exploration by Land.* New York: New Discovery Books/UNESCO Publishing, 1993.

Waldron, Arthur. *The Great Wall of China: From History to Myth.* Cambridge, England: Cambridge University Press, 1990.

Further Reading and Websites

All About the Great Wall of China
<http://www.enchantedlearning.com/subjects/greatwall/allabout.html>
This website includes a brief history of the Great Wall and a link to radar
pictures taken from space.

Baldwin, Robert F. *Daily Life in Ancient and Modern Beijing.* Minneapolis:
Runestone Press, 1999.
Rich details and vibrant illustrations reveal the culture and history of Beijing,
including the building of the capital's part of the Great Wall.

Behnke, Alison. *China in Pictures.* Minneapolis: Lerner Publications
Company, 2003.
This organized, fact-filled volume provides older readers with information on
all aspects of Chinese history, culture, geography, and economic activities.

Mann, Elizabeth. *The Great Wall. New York: Mikaya Press, 1997.*
Geared toward middle-grade readers, this history of the building of the Great
Wall describes the conflict between the Chinese and the northern nomadic
tribes that led to the wall's construction. The book is filled with maps,
timelines, photographs, and excellent illustrations, including a center foldout.

McNeese, Tim. *The Great Wall of China.* San Diego, CA: Lucent, 1997.
This history of the Great Wall, written for older readers, discusses the reasons
for the wall's construction, as well as the techniques used to build it.

Schneider, Mical. *Between the Dragon and the Eagle.* Minneapolis:
Carolrhoda Books, Inc., 1997.
This historical novel, set in A.D. 100 during the Han dynasty, traces the
journey of a bolt of silk from China to Italy along the Silk Road.

Secrets of the Great Wall
<http://www.discovery.com/stories/history/greatwall/greatwall.html>
This website is packed with information about the influence of the Great
Wall on Chinese history.

Stewart. Whitney. *Deng Xiaoping. Leader in a Changing China.*
Minneapolis: Lerner Publications Company, 2001.
Traces the life of the Chinese leader throughout a century of tumultuous
change.

Index

Lesley A. DuTemple has written more than a dozen books for young readers, including many award-winning titles such as her biography *Jacques Cousteau,* winner of the National Science Teachers Association/Children's Book Council Outstanding Science Trade Books for Children. After graduating from the University of California, San Diego, she attended the University of Utah's Graduate School of Architecture, where she concentrated in design and architectural history. The creator of the **Great Building Feats** series, she believes, "There's a human story behind every one of these building feats, and those stories are just as amazing as the projects themselves."

Photo Acknowledgments

All attempts have been made to contact the copyright holder(s) of the images in this book. If your image appears without proper credit, please contact Lerner Publishing Group.

© Keren Su/CORBIS, pp. 1, 42–43; © Bettmann/CORBIS, pp. 2–3, 55; © Dean Conger/CORBIS, pp. 4–5, 73; © North Wind Picture Archives, pp. 7 (N. Carter), 52–53; © China Stock, pp. 8, 8–9 (© Dennis Cox), 22, 25, 28, 34–35 (© Dennis Cox), 37 (© Liu Liqun), 42, 44 (© Dennis Cox), 46, 48 (© Li Shaobai), 49 (© Ru Suichu), 50 (© Liu Liqun), 52, 54 (© Christopher Liu), 56, 57 (© Li Shaobai), 59, 60 (© Liu Liqun), 66, 66–67 (© Li Shaobai), 71 (© Li Shaobai); Syndics of Cambridge University Library, p. 10; Cultural Relics Publishing House, Beijing, pp. 11, 39, 45, 47, 63; NASA, p. 13; © AFP/CORBIS, p. 16; © The Art Archive/Bibliothèque Nationale de Paris, p. 27; China National Public Import & Export Corporation, p. 29; Minneapolis Public Library and Information Center, p. 40 (both); Chhi Chhi Thu Shuo, p. 61 (top); Lateran Museum, Rome, pp. 64–65; © The Art Archive/Private Collection, p. 68; © Hulton-Deutsch Collection/CORBIS, p. 69; © Brown Brothers, p. 70; © CORBIS, p. 72. Maps and illustrations by Laura Westlund, pp. 6, 14, 20, 41, 58, 61 (bottom), 62, 64.

Cover photos are by: © Bettmann/CORBIS (front) and © North Wind Picture Archives (back).